Mandala Me Heart Coloring Book

PK Burian

Cover Illustrated by KP Azeltine

ISBN 13: 978-1523807468

ISBN 10: 1523807466

About The Author

PK Burian loved coloring as a child. She colored and loved to draw throughout her teens and college years. As a parent, she taught her daughters coloring and crafts. She couldn't be happier that adults are returning to an activity that once brought her and them such joy.

A writer of romance, young adult paranormal, middle-grade mystery, and picture books, she is happy to bring coloring books to adults, teens, and children.

You can find PK Burian at pkburian.com and pkburiancoloringbooks.com

LOVE

LOVE

LOVE

LOVE

LOVE

LOVE

LOVE

LOVE

LOVE

LOVE

LOVE

Go to: **pkburian.com or**

pkburiancoloringbooks.com

For more Mandala Me Coloring Books look for:

Mandala Me Beautiful
Mandala Me Animals
Mandala Me Paisley
Mandala Me Paisley Pretty
Mandala Me Love
Mandala Me Hearts

And for kids:

Animals of the Forest
Bears, Bears, Bears Coloring Book
Bears, Bears, Bears Activity Book
Birds of a Feather
Butterflies Everywhere
Happy Farm Animals
My Favorite Pet

More coming soon!

35361710R00031

Made in the USA
Middletown, DE
29 September 2016